Divination Rules

Divination Rules

100 TIPS FOR FLAWLESS FORTUNE-TELLING

CATHARINE ALLAN

STERLING ETHOS
New York

STERLING ETHOS
New York

Text © 2024 Catharine Allan
Illustrations © 2024 Union Square & Co., LLC

ISBN 978-1-4549-4550-5
ISBN 978-1-4549-4551-2 (e-book)

Library of Congress Control Number: 2024933134

For information about custom editions, special sales, and premium
purchases, please contact specialsales@unionsquareandco.com.

Printed in China

2 4 6 8 10 9 7 5 3 1

unionsquareandco.com

Cover and interior design by Renée Bollier
Cover and interior illustrations by Vero Escalante

— · ☽☽○☾☾ · —

This book is dedicated to all the experiences that shaped me and gave rise to the exploration of the great mysteries. To Shelly, my childhood neighbor for showing me the Magic 8 Ball, to my parents who never interfered with my spiritual path, and to all those who, like me, have followed their inner guidance despite the resistance.

Contents

Introduction

Divination has been in play cross-culturally and across time for centuries. It is just part of human nature itself to want to know why things are happening the way they are, explore strange phenomena, and peer into the potential future. There is written evidence of ancient Mesopotamians using divination as early as the second millennium BCE. It has been used all over the world, especially in Egypt, Greece, Italy, and China. It survives despite all attempts to suppress it by religious movements over the centuries. Why would something persist this long under adversity if it didn't have merit? It serves to calm us in the face of uncertainty, and it offers possibilities—whether they happen or not—and gets us thinking creatively and strategically about life. It's a way of coping with the unknown at its most reductive, and it's a spiritual practice connecting us to the Divine at its height.

One of my earliest memories of divination was dangling a needle and thread and letting it swing back and forth or in circles over the palm of my hand, which supposedly predicted how many children one would have, as well as whether they would be boys or girls. I distinctly remember it worked with my mom, circling first for a daughter, then swinging back and forth for a son, in the right order. I was mesmerized. How could this happen? Flash forward to the present day—by now, I've tried almost all the methods I've written about here, and a few have become my profession!

Though simple things like flipping a coin, shaking a Magic 8 Ball, or using an origami "fortune teller" are all considered divination, for methods that go beyond obvious one-word answers, it's best to follow some general guidelines—what I'm calling "rules" in this book. And while divination is necessarily an open-ended practice that rewards intuition, intention, and empathy, to accurately recognize and interpret the signs you will receive by using the methods described in this book is a lifelong practice that generations of seers have studied. It requires an understanding of ethics as well as a basic familiarity with the specific practice you are using. Therefore, I share my knowledge with you, that it may challenge your skills and provide you with direction when you receive symbolic answers, flashes of insight, and visions.

General Rules *and* Ethics

Always ask for permission before performing divination for someone else.

Consent is the name of the game for a healthy and ethical reading. If you walked around tapping people on the shoulder and saying, "I have a message for you," it would be a weird and invasive world. When the subject of a reading grants consent, they are allowing themselves to be receptive to the reader's message. Even when and if you are accurate about something in another person's life and want to share what you are feeling about it— even with good intentions—you can still cause dysregulation in someone badly if they are not ready and if they feel violated by the way it is communicated. Consent tells that the subject of a reading is ready to the best of their ability.

Take time to ground and center yourself before performing divination.

It's so important to learn how to ground yourself. Being grounded means you feel your feet are on the ground, you are in your body, and you are generally calm. When you are in this state, you will be more mindful and in the present moment, and you will be able to hear your intuition and higher self easily. With less "head noise" you will be a better interpreter and communicator of what you see. We want to be in a grounded state of mind, so we are not upset or reactive during a divination session, thereby running the risk of misinterpreting the information we receive or projecting our own issues onto our subject's life.

Be mindful of the language you use when interpreting divination messages.

Words really do matter. If you are asked a question about someone's love life and they are vulnerable and wanting to know what their partner truly feels about them—be *very* careful when it comes to the tone of voice you use and the words you choose. You never know what someone's mental or emotional state might be, so it's important to be tactful and sensitive. Love, or the lack of it, can push us to extremes at times, and this is usually when we come to divination for answers.

Generally, if we are given advice or a prediction of what is to come, many of us will remember and even obsess about it. If your words will resound in someone's mind for years to come, you'll want those words to be kind, positive, constructive, and empowering. This doesn't mean that you have to sugarcoat things either. There are ways to be honest *and* kind. It's also important to remember that divination answers are like mantras or spells in and of themselves. A symbol you see in a dream can mean one thing in one book, and something else in another. Interpretations and translations of texts can shift the way they are perceived and heard. So be aware of your language and tone. Above all, people always remember how you made them feel.

Divination is a sacred practice that should be treated with respect.

It's all too easy to think of divination as a game, but the questions it investigates are usually very emotional, and when we get a message or symbolic answer to something it can literally stop us in our tracks. Some of the predictions you will receive can stay with you for days, months, or even a lifetime, especially when they come true. So why would we play with our hearts and call this just a game? People can also be irreverent with the tools or the procedures (I think it's out of fear) to minimize the power of what might come through. But it's important to respect the proper ways to use these methods. Many were developed over centuries and have been the subject of generations of study and contemplation.

Never use divination as a way to manipulate or control others.

Once you feel the high of seeing a new way of looking at life, of having a sense of secret or ancient wisdom, it's easy to feel the power this can have to influence others. It's exciting for our personal development; it increases our self-expression and empowers us in our actions and decisions. And it can also stimulate the ego! Some will feel the surge of power to influence and be tempted to use it to manipulate circumstances.

If you know your tarot readings are influencing someone's decisions, and you think something needs to happen a certain way based on the cards, it's easy to justify your thinking with the cards and sway someone to see things as you do. This can be an innocent by-product of learning these arts, and you will outgrow it when you see it creates fear and resistance in those for whom you are reading (or, alternately, dependence on the cards or the reader). As we know, though, many will use these skills to manipulate and control. History books are full of examples of seers who were real and other mediums who were fakes. It is sadly very difficult for most to know which is which, particularly in the era of social media. People can take a quick, cheap course, and with slick marketing come off like a professional. There may not have been any real training with a mentor or guided practice with experts before becoming a professional, and there is rarely any counseling and psychology background.

Divination is very powerful thing when an answer or sign strikes you to the core. In the right hands, you will be guided to know how to frame the information you receive and help your subjects make peace with aspects of life that may be troubling them. To read and guide people with divination ethically, you need to know your craft well and have been trained by a mentor. You need to have empathy for others' feelings, and you have to transcend your own ego. A true medium, clairvoyant, astrologer, or healer must be able to do this.

Be open to receiving messages that may challenge your beliefs.

As your intuition gets stronger, and as your knowledge of divination becomes more refined, you will start to receive information and messages that challenge your core beliefs and ways of thinking about the world. You might ask a question and receive an answer that really disturbs you and leaves you conflicted for weeks. You have to be open to changing your paradigm to use divination. Otherwise, you will end up repackaging things you already believe or replaying old stories from your childhood. To hear something innovative, creative, and transcendent, you have to be receptive. The concepts and words that become part of your practice will surprise you as you grow. Welcome them!

Be mindful of your intentions when performing divination.

Your intentions matter and will set the tone for what you receive from your divination methods. Sometimes it isn't easy to identify your intentions before you ask your tarot a question or swing your pendulum. If you often feel frustrated by the answers you get, it could be a sign that your intentions aren't clearly defined. The divination tool will pick up on the energy of what you're truly sending out. For example, you ask, "What does my future mother-in-law think of me?" when your real question is, "Does she approve of me as his fiancée?" It's all in the same ballpark, but one is a general question asked while you're feeling nervous, and the second is specific and asked as you're prepared to accept honesty, so your divination tool will give you a corresponding answer. When answers are confusing or frustrating, try to refocus your intention and see if your tools speak to you louder. Usually, they will.

Be respectful of the divination traditions of other cultures.

You must be very conscious and careful of cultural appropriation along your journey. White sage is a medicine used by First Nations, and the use of it can be considered offensive if you are not Indigenous. While commodifying others' spiritual practices disrespects the medicine, the practice of our own ancestral traditions can be very powerful. On a cellular level, you will activate something to bring these traditions and herbs or divination tools into your life. These practices connect you to your ancestors.

However, in some cases the influences of our past lives present themselves as a strong attraction to a certain cultural path. This is where it gets tricky because sometimes this is calling you so strongly that if you don't follow it, you may create a blockage in your development. In these instances, you should delve into the practices of other cultures only once you have studied them and possess an authentic and deep respect for their history and traditions. Additionally, always practice with humility and restraint. This might mean you do it privately instead of putting photos on Instagram, and certainly not teaching it to anyone else. You would need to be accepted and acknowledged by that community before it's safe to use their ways.

Be mindful of the energy you bring to your divination practice.

When you do a reading for someone, you really need to know what energy is yours and what energy is theirs. Simple, but important: you need to be centered. If you are tired, own it. If you start by saying the other person seems to have low energy or is tired, check yourself first. Is that low energy yours? Are you projecting it, or is it truly what you are picking up from them? If you are grieving someone or something at the time you practice divination, be extra careful that you don't impose your own sadness, grief, fear, and pessimism onto the reading at hand, whether for yourself or the other person. It takes a certain degree of self-awareness to do this, but we can all strive to be more honest about where we're at before we begin any activity, so we can own it and integrate it.

Keep your divination tools and space clean and sacred.

There are many ways to cleanse and store your divination items. It can reflect your culture, or the conventional wisdom attached to the items you are using—it's up to you. Many believe you need black silk and a wooden box to store your tarot cards, for example, keeping them in a safe place out of the light as well. But it makes sense: placing your cards in a special cloth, bag, or box is a good idea to keep them free of dust in addition to protecting them from any negative energy.

However, in my opinion, your tarot bag doesn't have to be black silk. Another example: To cleanse your space, cards, or any other tool, many people recommend smudging them with sage. But you can also use cedar, juniper, palo santo, or other medicine from your culture. Alternately, you can simply hold the objects you wish to cleanse, moving them around through the smoke as it burns. Other people who have the training can cleanse their tools and space with Reiki as well. If you don't have Reiki training, you can cleanse and keep your space and tools sacred by visualization of light or sacred geometry. It might take time to be able to do this, but then you won't need to burn anything and can do it anywhere.

Use divination as a way to access higher states of consciousness.

The way you use divination is everything. If you ask yes or no questions about simple things, like whether someone will call you back, this is the level of answer you will get as well. If, on the other hand you ask a deeper or more complex question, you will get an answer that mirrors this. This is the way it works. So you can use divination to further your spiritual path and access higher states of consciousness. How? Ask things from your divination tool like, "How do I raise my level of self-awareness right now?" You can also use alternative methods like crystal ball gazing or other forms of scrying (gazing into any reflective object or surface) to allow yourself to go deeper into meditation, and through this, you will access higher states of awareness. Most of the divination tools you use can be a gateway to higher states of consciousness. It all depends on how you use them and what your intentions are.

Use divination as a way to explore your spiritual path and purpose.

Using divination to explore your path is great because you can experiment with so many modalities from many different eras and areas of the world. As you explore these paths, pay attention to which one makes the most sense, comes most easily, or fascinates you most to learn. You can gather a few different divination tools and meditate on them first. Ask your higher self to show you which method fits you best on your path at this time. Trust your dreams, intuition, and general feeling of aliveness when using each one to help you decide.

You don't have to use just one, but as you evolve you will be drawn to studying one in particular so you get to know it very well. The more you master it, the richer the experience and wisdom you will gain from it. You can use your methods to determine which tradition is right for you, by using them for a while and seeing which one draws you most. Questions about your spiritual purpose are often hard to answer for anyone. How do you sum up a lifetime in one purpose? You might want to break it down into chapters of your life by thinking about what your spiritual purpose or lesson is right now, and then ask qualifying questions to see how long that lesson will last. If you try to refine your questions along these huge topics, you can find meaningful answers and set goals more easily than trying to sum up your whole life at once.

Use divination to gain clarity and insight into complex situations.

Most of the divination methods you use have the capacity to take you much deeper into your interpretations of questions. You can read the one-word or one-line explanation of anything, but things are generally much deeper and more complex than that. We look to divination for insight. You might not receive the literal and complete answer to a situation, nor should you. Divination is more of a gateway to think in new ways. If, for example, you can't decide where to live and you encounter blue jays everywhere as you ponder this, you can investigate what blue jays mean, their nature, their habitat, and migration patterns, and this totem can show you the way over time. Totems are a complex practice, often unfolding over years of understanding. Be willing to go deeper, and honor the smallest detail.

Remember that coincidences aren't always coincidences.

Even Carl Jung agreed that synchronicity happens when coincidences are meaningful. These patterns connect us to the divine when we see virtually impossible things happen to us, especially when they happen close together in a specific order. For example, running into someone three times in one day randomly is an opportunity to meet this person and find out why the universe is connecting your paths right now. When we see angel numbers, sequences of repeated numbers that appear randomly as signs from the universe, especially if they appear multiple times throughout your day, this can also be a message that should be taken into account. Repeating numbers can help us validate our choices. If you suddenly start seeing 234 everywhere, on the clock, license plates, prices in the store, and then you're asked to show up for an interview and the address is 234, you can recognize the synchronicity and take it as a good omen. Thinking of someone just before they call is a fun and somewhat common intuitive experience, but what if you take it to the next level and this seems to happen with you and a certain person over and over? You would likely take this as proof of your strong bond and pay attention to this relationship in a slightly different way than others, looking for more meaning. Always pay attention to synchronous events.

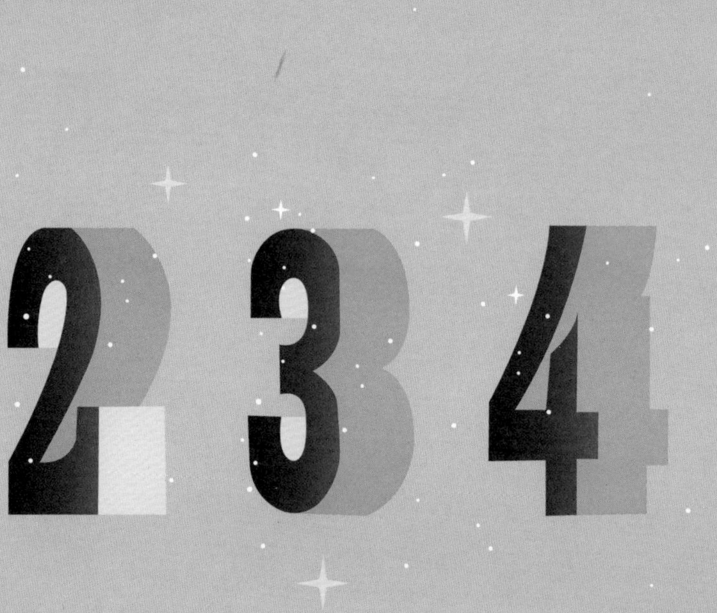

Use divination as a way to connect with your ancestors and spirit guides.

You can also use divination to access your spirit guides and ask them for signs of what tools to use by meditating. During this meditation, if you have a vision of ancient China, your spirit guides might be encouraging you to study feng shui or face reading, and you can ask your intuition if your spirit guide is from there. Divination tools come from all over the world, so each one could potentially lead you to ancient Egypt, Greece, or the Celts. Start with identifying which tool can geolocate your spirit guide.

Another amazing thing you can do to connect is to ask your guide to give you tangible signs when in deep meditation. Perhaps you begin to see feathers everywhere. Feathers tell you which bird is guiding you and give you the chance to observe the flight patterns of the birds around you. Guides can speak to you this way.

Use divination to tap into your intuition and psychic abilities.

By using divination tools on a regular basis, you will begin to open your intuition naturally, and your psychic abilities will grow. Allowing yourself to be open and receptive is a crucial part of divination, so it's important to have experiences that open you up and surprise you. The more you learn to allow feelings, words, and images to flow freely, and to trust them, the more you will become immersed in the modality, and the more details you will receive. Another practice that helps to build your intuitive muscles is to start using divination for others. As you begin to do more readings—whether you use tarot, pendulums, tea leaves, or animal totem stories—you will see an increase in your abilities, and the depth and range of what you pick up will increase.

Be open to receiving messages from unexpected sources.

Messages come from a wide range of sources! You might ask the universe if you should leave your job and seek a new one. You keep waiting for a clear, undeniable voice that tells you what to do, but instead you get ads for employment agencies when you scroll through Instagram, or you meet five people who left their jobs recently within a single week, or you haven't watched a movie in a month and the one you choose turns out to have a main character who quits a job and reinvents their life. These are all valid signs. You might be consulting the tarot and astrology about your love life over and over, wondering if love will enter your life, and get a variety of answers to ponder; then you start seeing hearts all over the place. Your latte arrives with a heart on it, you see chalk hearts drawn on the sidewalk—these are signs to trust love is all around you.

Sometimes the answer you have been seeking will be a comment someone makes on the sidewalk passing by. They don't know you or your circumstances and casually say something to you in passing that awakens you. Many times, our children and pets speak to us and give us the signs we seek. The main thing is to understand the nature of these messages; this is called synchronicity, a language of patterns that give you answers.

Remember that divination is not a game or a party trick.

This one is really important to understand well. Even when someone asks seemingly casual questions about their future, career, or relationship, they are allowing themselves to be vulnerable with you, or they wouldn't ask. On this basis alone, we know that divination is not a game. The feelings and mental health of others matters, and if we act as if the art of divination is a game, we run the risk of treating other people's emotions too casually. There is great responsibility to others when we learn these arts and have influence on their perception and decision-making.

Tarot

Choose the tarot deck that inspires you most.

You are going to be looking at your deck *a lot* so the imagery absolutely has to call to you. Many people will tell you to start with a classic Rider-Waite deck, but that is not always necessary. You can get one to learn the basic meanings of the cards as Waite interpreted them, but know that there are other ways to understand the very same cards in other tarot decks. Most decks use the Rider-Waite as a template for general meanings and then reinterpret them slightly. Go with your gut when making your decision, and choose a deck that inspires you the most.

Learn your deck before giving a reading.

When you begin, it's normal for you to be very excited about reading for yourself or your friends. However, remember that people take your words and interpretations to heart. They ask for readings when they are more vulnerable than usual, so it's important to know your basics and give some serious thought to the impact your readings may have on someone before you start offering predictions. Far too many people are buying tarot cards and taking quickie courses, but in truth, it takes about a year to really absorb the seventy-eight cards well enough to begin to read.

Your readings will still work for you even if you don't follow classic superstitions.

One of those superstitions is that your tarot deck must be gifted to you versus you buying your own deck. This really doesn't matter! It's hard to give a good reading with a deck you don't feel connected to, so if the tarot is a gift but you don't resonate with it, then it won't be helpful. Another superstition is to keep your cards in a special box and wrapped in black silk. This also doesn't matter. However, your cards *do* need to be treated as sacred tools and have some sort of ritual associated with the way you store and cleanse them. You can choose to store them in silk or a wooden box, or you might choose to keep them in a leather bag and a specific drawer instead. It's up to you. Superstitions might initially help you form a ritual, but the power isn't in the superstition itself—it's in the understanding of the sacredness.

Open the reading in a positive way.

Put your clients at ease by asking how they are doing and chatting about light topics for a few minutes before getting started. Most people are anxious when they come to a reading, so a couple minutes of easy conversation can help everyone breathe and settle into it. You can start with open-ended questions such as, "What brings you to a reading today?" or invite them to ask you any questions about how you work before you open the cards. You can even ask if they are nervous and actively reassure them for a bit. Many people are scared the cards will say something negative so anything you do to help people relax will lead to a better reading. Once you begin, listening is very reassuring and positive to most. If you see something in their cards right away that might be a sensitive topic, try to bring it up in a gentle way at first and let them open up to you. This will show you whether they are ready to receive the message you see. You can gradually bring up the tougher things as trust builds during the rest of the session.

Preparing the space before a reading is essential.

You will need a private and quiet place where you won't be inter-
rupted. Next you will want to make sure the space is clean and
has fresh air. You can burn a candle, incense, or sage to cleanse
and bless the space before you begin. Some people may use Reiki
or sound to clear the energy before a session, and some may
prefer to chant, say a prayer, or recite a mantra beforehand. You
can choose any method as long as it gives a sense of clearing the
space to make it sacred before you open up the reading. Privacy
is very important for readings as well. You must minimize all
distractions and possible interruptions to the reading, as they
can be upsetting to you and to the sitter. When emotional and
sensitive information comes through, no one wants it cut in half
by someone bursting in a door or by loud music. Privacy and
silence, or calming music, are a big part of setting the stage and
preparing the space.

Reading for yourself is difficult but possible!

Why is it so hard to get a good reading for yourself? It's quite simply because you are too emotionally attached to the out-comes, so it's more difficult to be objective. However, there is a way to get a glimpse of the truth from the cards if you try a couple of things. First, try looking for patterns in your readings, including repeated cards drawn for questions about similar issues or in general readings. If you do a three-card reading representing the past, present, and future on a daily basis, you may start to see the cards change in order, then disappear. This correlates to your life events. Watch what happens in your life and see which card a particular event might have corresponded to—over time you will get a feel for which cards corresponded to your actual life events.

Another strategy for getting real readings when you do them for yourself is to meditate on the cards you draw, rather than expecting fast, concrete answers. Try choosing one card for your situation and then placing it where you can see it for a few days, allowing you to sense whatever comes up. After you have spent some time with this card, you may get a little peek into your fate. Remember, though—sometimes it's just easier to consult a professional! Interpretation of the cards can be by the book or intuitive. Most of us start off learning from the tarot booklet that comes with a deck, and we rely on it as we memorize the traditional meanings of each card.

You can expect it to take up to a year to memorize all seventy-eight cards, but truly understanding them can take much longer. It's an evolution. The more readings you give, the more you will notice that sometimes the booklet descriptions don't match your intuition about the querent's question. So what do you do? The best-case scenario is to learn your tarot cards well enough to give the traditional meaning, and then add your intuition to the mix. This will give you lots to ponder and interpret if they seem contradictory, but this is where you start to give more rich and accurate readings.

Ask clear questions.

If you want to get a good answer, you need a good question. It's normal for people to occasionally be unclear in their desire to tap into their future, but a vague question will often lead to a very general answer. If a person asks, "What is my future?" that question is way too broad to answer. It implies summing up an entire life! If instead they ask, "What does the future hold for me in the next three months?" there is now a parameter that helps interpret the answer more clearly, and there is the potential to go into some detail. Instead of asking, "What is going on in my relationship?" a better question to ask might be, "Is this relationship for my highest good?" or "Is this relationship truly mutual?" or "What can I do to improve my relationship with so-and-so?" All these questions will allow you to get more specific answers.

There are ethics to respect when reading for others.

Consent—always ask permission before giving a reading to someone. It sounds obvious, but many people bypass this, inboxing others with solicitous messages to seduce them. Want to be sure you are a good reader? Ask permission. Confidentiality—what you see and say to someone during a reading must stay with you. You are the keeper of confidences as a tarot reader. Honesty—say what you sense as gently and truthfully as you can while being sensitive to the person receiving it. Personal responsibility—encouraging people and engendering hope is essential when giving a reading. Your words and the overall feeling you give to someone about their life will have an impact, so leave people feeling hopeful and able to change their situation.

It is completely up to you to choose whether or not you read reversed cards.

People are often of two camps on this issue. Some readers always use reversed cards and meanings, and some never read them reversed. Reversed cards mostly have negative meanings, so there is a big debate in the tarot community about whether or not to use them. A reading could have so many reversed cards that the querent might feel hopeless afterward. Other readers might keep all cards upright, unless by fluke (or, some may say, destiny) a card is reversed; it would then be considered significant.

Try both for an extended amount of time and see if the readings improve for you. Some people feel that if they use the cards upright all the time and then one randomly comes up reversed, it's an omen. Others feel if there are too many reversals, there might be interference in the reading by lower spirits. And finally, others channel the tarot cards and feel that whatever the orientation, the meanings will be clear regardless. How you read the cards is a very personal choice, and it is wholly up to you.

Closing off a reading properly is important.

So many times after a reading full of questions and emotions, the subject of your reading can feel that the end has been chopped off abruptly or that their questions haven't been fully answered. It's important to prevent these feelings by bringing closure to the interaction so that the person you are reading for, your querent, feels that they have received clear guidance. Like anything else in life, when things fade out or feelings are cut off suddenly, it causes us to linger, rehashing the situation, doubting ourselves, or feeling insecure—none of which are the goal of a good reading, which is to bring light and clarity.

A simple way to give closure is to declare when the reading is complete, then recap the important points for the person to focus on going forward. You can leave them with something to work on, a goal, or a reassuring thought. You can also lead a moment of quiet, guiding your client with a few deep breaths. Or you can invite the person to share how they feel about the reading overall before you close the session. It doesn't matter which of these things you do, as long as it feels positive and results in a clear pause or shift from the energy of the reading. It's like driving fast on the highway and gently putting on the brakes before you shift to a residential street. You create a bridge to call attention to the fact that the reading is now done, but you're still there for a bit of support at the end.

After the reading has concluded, don't answer any additional questions because this opens the reading again. Instead, you can offer a follow-up session or suggest things the querent can do to resolve any lingering questions. Some people like to use markers such as sound—a gong or tingshas, or burning incense at the end of a session to shift the energy. Readings awaken the querent and encourage them to explore their fears and insecurities, so once the rabbit hole is open it can be hard to close it. Think of a peaceful ritual that helps you and the querent accept the closure of the reading.

Astrology

Astrology is an amazing tool for self-knowledge.

Whether you believe in astrology or not, its usefulness to break down aspects of our personalities and dive deeper into our own psyches is undeniable. Asking yourself who you are versus how you present yourself to the outside world can be a ground-breaking tool for self-awareness and mastery. To ask yourself what your core emotional needs are and then to respect them will bring consciousness to any relationship and will help you understand what you need to be truly happy. To give you just one example of how you can understand your life by investigating the movements of the planets, the locations of Venus and Mars in your natal chart can give you insight into the dynamics between what you want (Venus) and how you go about getting it (Mars). If Venus is in Gemini and Mars is in Sagittarius, they oppose each other. You want to do everything with everyone and stay curious and adaptable—flirting, socializing, networking, multitasking, brainstorming. Mars in Sagittarius, by contrast, is surer and more singular. Think of shooting a single arrow long and far.

These two planets can help each other out if Venus in Gemini can get clear on one thing it wants (which is very hard!) so that Mars in Sagittarius can go big or go home to make it happen. If it stays scattered or is too diversified, Mars in Sagittarius will be very frustrated and restless. But if Venus is in Cancer and Mars is in Scorpio, this is much easier to manage because both are water signs and will support each other. Both desire depth, emotional expression, and spiritual and intuitive aspects to life. So it's just a matter of getting these two aspects of your personality to work together! This is just the tip of the iceberg of what you can see about yourself through the birth chart. It's a brilliant way to pose questions to yourself throughout life, and it provides a lens through which you can see life to help give you some objectivity.

Rising signs are who you are outwardly in life.

Your rising, or ascendant, sign is the way you show your personality to the world. Sometimes your ascendant gives a totally different impression to the world than when people really get to know you. The more concerned you are about your outward presentation to the world or what people think of you, the more active your ascendant will be. You might bring this side of you especially to your professional life since you protect your heart or privacy there. However, you might have planets very close to the ascendant that can make it very hard to conceal from others how you feel or who you are. For example, if your moon is positioned close to your ascendant, your emotions will always show to others. If Uranus is on your ascendant, others will see all your quirks, including your rebellious side. Making peace with your rising sign and what effect it has on your life will greatly help you going forward.

Moon signs reliably show your true needs.

This might be one of the most important pieces of information to understand about yourself. The moon represents your deep emotions, your relationship with your mother and her qualities, and your subconscious—dreams, intuitions, mysterious feelings, and past lives. When your natal moon sign is happy and has its needs met, you are generally happy and successful. If you rail against it, you will always be frustrated or depressed and anxious, or even feel betrayed somehow. If you have the moon in Libra for example, you *need* things to be as fair as possible. You need art and harmony. You need romance and beauty. People can call you what they want, but these are "needs," not just "wants." If you have the moon in Leo, you *need* some aspect of life where you shine and get the spotlight. You need some drama, theater, and a flair of self-expression. This is the closeted performer who needs to find a way to shine behind the scenes.

Your astrology chart mapped onto the global map shows your best places to live, love, and succeed.

Astro cartography is so fascinating. You can trace your Venus line for example, which will be a long, curved line passing through the globe, to show you where you might find good friendships, love, and to be liked in general. Your Mars line will show places of action but also possible conflict and danger. Check yours and see if any of your favorite destinations match a planetary line!

Compatibility goes deeper than sun signs.

Astrological compatibility is highly complex, but there are a few things you can check for that will really help you determine if you and another person are a good match. Look at Mercury for intellectual compatibility and communication ease or issues. Make sure something in your partner's chart supports your moon sign. For example, if you have a Scorpio moon, you will benefit from someone with their sun, Mercury, Venus, Mars, or Jupiter in Scorpio, Cancer, or Pisces because they are also water signs and therefore support each other.

Next, look at Venus signs to see if you want the same things. Check to see if your Venus signs are compatible with each other, and with your sun, moon, Mercury, or rising sign in the aspects they make to each other. Beneficial aspects would be 120 degrees or 60 degrees. Venus will bring love and admiration in that instance and will help resolve any conflicts. The next important thing is to look at Mars. Mars can bring passion and vitality to a relationship, but also conflict. If your Mars signs are compatible, it means you have similar energy levels and take action in similar ways. Jupiter will expand anything it touches, so ideally, you want good aspects here to promote positivity and growth. Saturn is the last personal planet to assess. Saturn is the bringer of life lessons and structure, so it's not an easy influence, but in order for there to be any kind of longevity in a relationship, it is essential that there are learning opportunities and enough grit to stick together.

Astrological transits are predictive.

Transits are the passage of the current planets as they align with your birth chart. Every year the sun will touch everything in your chart and highlight it. Other transits are very long and will only travel through a portion of your chart—like Neptune or Pluto. The moon will touch everything in your chart each month. When you see a planet aligning in the skies with a planet in your chart, you can count on some sort of event or awakening to occur. Depending on the planets, the aspects they activate, and the houses they pass through, you can make some significant predictions. Generally, if a major planet conjuncts (falls on the same degree as) your ascendant/descendant axis, there will be a lot of life changes. This is the core dichotomy between you and others, your independence, and your relationship commitments. You might feel very torn between the two when a planet transits here, especially if that planet is known to bring luck (Jupiter), passion and aggression (Mars), restriction (Saturn), or unpredictability and restlessness (Uranus). Being aware of your transits gives you a framework to help you make more strategic choices. The Midheaven determines your career direction and your public persona. The Midheaven in astrology is the top of the chart; think of 12:00 o'clock. The sign of your Midheaven tells you the kind of career you would be good at and like, where you can shine, and where you might be publicly recognized. Even without a career, we all have a reputation and some social standing. This area of the chart is where you might get an idea of what that looks like. If you have your Midheaven in Leo, you are here to stand out, be onstage, lead meetings, run your own company, or be self-employed. You will want to be publicly visible and get recognition for your pursuits, and you will be sensitive to how people perceive you, because Leo wants to be loved and adored. This could be anything from an actor, CEO, or a beloved kindergarten teacher. Some famous examples are Robin Willaims, Vladimir Putin, and Katy Perry.

If you have your Midheaven in Scorpio, by contrast, you do not want public attention at all. You want to accomplish, but behind the scenes, or be known as private or mysterious. You might be drawn to psychology, research, or detective work, or as a specialist who is known by word-of-mouth recommendations as opposed to public advertisements. The exception to this would be someone who uses the spotlight and reputation to bring up the taboo subjects we want to avoid. Some famous examples are Jane Fonda, Dustin Hoffman, and Bono. Keep in mind these are celebrities, so look at the quality of their career compared to the Leo Midheavens. When you see certain planets near your Midheaven they also tell you what kind of reputation and career you might have. If you have Mercury close to your Midheaven by degree, then communications will be a big part of your work— possibly writing, editing, public speaking, working in a library, etc. If you have the sun near your Midheaven, it is a beautiful aspect that you are here to shine and be known, and there will be successes, as well as many responsibilities that go with it.

35

Mercury retrograde is about reflection.

Mercury retrograde has quickly become a mainstream topic. We warn against signing documents, caution against verbal misunderstandings, and expect accidents or overlooked details. The planet doesn't have any particular superpower over us, as much as we would love to blame it for our absentmindedness. It's more that retrogrades push our awareness inward and make us more reflective, sentimental, or indecisive. You might feel more spaced out during this influence, or your mind may be on too many things and therefore you miss a detail that can cost you. So, when you see Mercury retrogrades announced throughout the year—three times a year for three weeks at a time—don't put your life completely on hold; just pay extra attention to the way you communicate and be mindful of your agreements, and all should be well.

Aspects are everything.

You might have a well-placed planet in its sign or house, but if the aspects to it are challenging it will all play out differently. Similarly, if you have a difficult planet in a potent part of the chart, like your ascendant, it can be well aspected and soften its blow. The aspects are the mathematical angles each planet makes to other planets and house cusps. If you have Venus on your Midheaven or career/visibility fame angle, this is a great boost to your ability to be promoted and seen. If that same Venus has Saturn squaring it, then there will be visibility, but

also challenges to it—like someone questioning your methods or reputation, for example. Aspects tell us the relationship of each planet to the others and let us know if they are working together or against each other. Since we have many planets to consider, and sometimes multiple aspects to one planet, the complexity of the chart is shown in understanding them. It also plays a big part in compatibility with others too. Planetary dignity can determine if you display to positive or difficult traits of a sign. Each planet has a dignity or distinction, whether it is in its best placement or its worst. First we have the ruler of the sign, such as the sun ruling Leo, the moon ruling Cancer, Virgo and Gemini ruling Mercury, etc. The next is detriment, which is the opposite of the rulership. Therefore, the sun is in its detriment in Aquarius, the moon is in detriment in Capricorn, etc. After that we have exaltation, where this planet energy expresses its best traits. For example, Mars is exalted in Capricorn because its normally impulsive or destructive ways transform into productivity, work, and self-control. Venus is exalted in Pisces because the desire nature in us is expressed with compassion and consideration for all versus the self. Finally, we have the detriment position where the planet expresses the shadow side of the sign. Mars is in its detriment in Cancer because it needs to act and be direct when in balance, and Cancer makes it conflict avoidant and therefore overly sentimental and manipulative to get what it wants; think of guilt trips. It can help us in our growth to see what distinction our personal planets have so we can be mindful of what areas we can improve upon.

Solar returns predict the year ahead.

Every year the sun returns to the same place as when you were born. At this moment we cast a chart, like a snapshot of the heavens for the personal new year ahead starting at your birthday. The solar return chart will have the sun at the same degree as your birth, but all the rest will be different. You will have an ascendant for that year and a moon sign for that year. It's a more accurate way to predict what may happen in the year ahead. We do this by seeing the configuration of planets for that year as if it's a separate person born on your birthday. This shows us the planets, aspects, and houses they affect for that year. After that we compare them to the natal chart and see what is affecting you—it's like a relationship compatibility between your birth date and your solar return. From this we get a good idea of what parts of your life will be highlighted and at the timing. The nodal axis of the moon shows your past life and your life direction now.

Nodal astrology is fascinating and so helpful. Let's explain what it is first before getting into how to interpret it. If you drew the path of the moon around Earth you wouldn't get a perfect circle, you would get an ellipse. If you drew the ellipse of the moon around Earth and then the horizon line through Earth at the time you were born, the two points where they intersect are your north node and south node. The north node is the direction your life is going in now and the changes you need to make for things to grow and manifest. Most of us cling to our south node thinking and behaviors, which represent our past lives and what was very familiar in the last life. These are our fallback behaviors when in distress. When we heal and grow, we start to adopt the thinking and behaviors of our north node and life starts to move forward and flow easily. At first it feels completely weird and awkward, but over time you will see it is true. For example, if your north node is in Libra and your south node is in Aries, you will be used to being solitary, bold, impulsive, warrior minded, fiery temperament, and sometimes selfish in good ways and in bad ways. The Libra north node asks you to grow by being in partnership, balancing your needs and others' needs, and being more passive for the sake of reason and cohesion within a group or family. It will ask you to suppress the impulsive and courageous action and instead opt for mediation and compromise. If you are feeling stuck in your life, it can help to research and reflect on your north node sign and start to adopt or emulate more of that sign's traits.

Your birth time is essential for chart calculation.

Every four minutes the sun changes a degree on the horizon. This means if your birth time is even a few minutes off it will change the interpretation. Most of the time it's not too significant if you are off by five to ten minutes, but once in a while that one degree of shift means a planet falls into a different house or your moon sign or rising sign will be different. Astrology is very precise and sensitive. Try to get your accurate birth time from an archive in the hospital where you were born. Once the birth time is accurate and the chart is cast, you can see important timing for events and chapters of life that change as transiting planets enter or exit a house.

For example, if Venus enters your fifth house (which it will because Venus moves fairly quickly through the signs) you will enjoy a period of increased playfulness and creativity, attract dates or new love, and increase your self-expression. However, if it's Pluto entering a house, the impact can last for twenty or thirty years. This influence will bring about a huge transformation in that area of your life for many years, so it's worth knowing.

Saturn returns are important evaluation points in life.

Saturn is the planet of life lessons, structure, and time. We won't escape our life lessons so it's better to understand what they are and work on them. Saturn also rewards us when we have learned them. Every seven years it will make a square—a hard aspect—to itself in our chart, so we feel tested. It's a marker to see how we are doing with that lesson! The Saturn return is a time when it has completed a full rotation and returns to the place it was when we were born. This takes about twenty-nine and a half years. When we have our first one, we feel suddenly older, responsibility sinks in, and the area of our lives highlighted in this lesson will likely feel like a restriction. We have a second one around sixty years old, to see how much we've learned its lessons. Every seven years in between we get a challenge or nudge. It's worth knowing what our Saturn lesson is and when these markers come so we can work with it instead of feeling trapped by it. You can find your Saturn placement by doing your birth chart or looking at an ephemeris. Outer planets determine generational factors. The outer planets are considered to be Saturn, Uranus, Neptune, and Pluto. Saturn's passage is two and a half years, so it starts to give a feel or color to a group of people born close together with similar life lessons, strengths, and restrictions. We can define this by calling it our peer group.

When it comes to Uranus, it lasts seven years in one sign. It takes eighty-four years to complete the zodiac, so we might live through its complete cycle or not. This makes it significant because Uranus is the rebel or upheaval force where something previously agreed upon as the norm gets shaken up like a series of earthquakes and causes a shift in society. We all have Uranus in our own charts, so it points to where we will make such an impact or have to deal with it in our own lives. Neptune's transits are around fourteen years. In a life span, one planet staying this long in one sign's influence starts to color the tastes, thinking, and lessons of a generation.

Finally, Pluto, the longest transit of them all, can last anywhere from twelve years up to thirty-one years! When Pluto was in Taurus from 1852 to 1883, the world saw many difficult financial transformations, including those of Karl Marx. From January 2024 up to March 2043 it will be in Aquarius. This means huge societal changes to come. It is well worth your time to see where in your chart Pluto will be affecting you because it lasts so long.

Traditional Predictive Tools

Consider all aspects of the hand, not just the lines.

Most of the time when we think about palmistry, we think of the love line or the life line and want to know how long we will live, what events might show up along the way, or if we will marry and when. However, there are many things to consider with palm reading. For example, there are other symbols that show up, such as triangles, stars, circles, and minor lines we don't think of as much, like the fate line. We also need to look at the overall shape of the hand, the length of the fingers and thumb in comparison, and the fleshiness or flatness of the hand and the mounds. All of these show the personality and the health of a person. For example, if your thumb can bend almost backward it means you are extravagant and will spend too much money on a whim. If your pinky finger separates from your other fingers, it means you are an independent thinker.

Angel numbers appear
when your intuition opens up.

Do repetitive and sequential numbers mean anything when you
keep seeing them? YES! Does it mean something if you keep
seeing 1:11 on the clock versus 4:44 or 2:34? YES! Each number
has a meaning. Some books assign meanings to almost any
repeating number you see. Some numbers are angel numbers or
master numbers. When you see 1:11, 2:22, or 3:33, these are master
numbers that indicate very high energy is around you. They also
mean your intuition and even psychic ability is opening up.
Almost everyone who starts seeing the numbers tells me they
also start connecting to their higher self and their dreams,
seeing clairvoyant visions, or otherwise experiencing an
increase in perception. If you keep seeing a number that isn't
a master number but repeats for you personally, it can be a
sign of a few things. Your spirit guide might choose that time
because of something that happened to you around that time.
For instance, if an important life event happened to you at
10:26 a.m., then that number repeating can be your personal sign
to pay attention.

Names carry vibrational numbers.

Every letter has a number value to it. We can add the numbers of our names to get a numerological vibration. You can do your first name and last name separately to see your individual vibration and the family name vibration. You can add them both together to combine your energy to the family line and see what insight it gives you. We start with "A" and "1," and go from 1 to 9 with each letter, then start again until the whole alphabet is assigned. If we look at John Lennon, J = 1, O = 6, H = 8, N = 5, so John is 1 + 6 + 8 + 5 = 20 or 2. Lennon would be L = 3, E = 5, N = 5, N = 5, O = 6, N = 5, so 3 + 5 + 5 + 5 + 6 + 5 = 29 or 11. His last name is the master number 11. His entire name then adds to 49, which breaks down to 13 or 4. This corresponds to the Death card in the tarot. You can see John by itself is a 2—partnerships, dualities, intuition. His last name is a master number 11—open to the spirit realms, manifestor, very psychic. Together they make a transformational combination, and his life certainly fits this in many ways.

There is more than one way to add your life path number.

Your life path number determines your energy in terms of personality and expression, what motivates you, and what you are here to do in this lifetime. Most books will tell you to determine your life path number by writing down your full birthday and adding one digit at a time, then reducing that number to a single digit, unless it is 11 or 22. It would look like this: July 23, 1971, would be $7+2+3+1+9+7+1=30$, which breaks down to a 3 life path. If you add it in another way, sometimes it gives a different result, and if that means you have a master number (11, 22, 33) it's worth trying! If you add the day to the month, then add that to the year and break it down, you would get: $7+23=30$, $30+1971=2001$; $2+0+0+1$ is still a number 3 life path. Try this with a different birthday: July 17, 1969. The first method would be $7+1+7+1+9+6+9=40$, which breaks down to a 4 life path. The second method would be $7+17=24$, then $24+1969=1993$, which adds to a 22 life path! 22 also breaks down to a 4, but if you have a master number in your life path it makes a huge difference to how you feel and how you can go about getting what you desire. Try both and see.

Create parameters or a container before throwing your lots.

Cleromancy is an ancient divination practice that centers on throwing objects. Stones, runes, yarrow stalks, or dice made of bones were thrown throughout the Middle East, Africa, and Europe, especially Germany and Scandinavia. Before casting lots to ask a question, a circle might have been drawn, and a bowl or container was often used to contain these objects. Whatever landed inside it was interpreted. Yarrow stalks were used to interpret the *I Ching* trigrams. Runes, symbols drawn onto small stones, have been popular throughout time, as well as dice made of bones.

The "container," if it isn't a physical boundary for the runes or stones to land in, can be the parameters of the reading. Questions like, "What is in store for my career," are parameters, as opposed to open-ended and general tosses of the dice. Grids can be drawn with quadrants for different aspects of life, and then the interpretation can be made based on the sector they land in, plus the number or symbol on the lot. If you've ever simply flipped a coin for heads or tails, you have practiced cleromancy.

Smudge or cleanse your runes before using.

As with any other divination tool, runes need to be cleansed between uses from different people or even between different questions you ask them. Since the runes are usually held in the palms firmly before they are thrown or individually chosen, a querent's energy is more likely to linger on them. You can cleanse them in a few ways. You can place them on their special cloth and pass smoke over them—usually sage, cedar, juniper, rosemary, or palo santo—or you can also hold them in the bag they come in and visualize light around yourself and the runes. When the previous energy is not cleared you will notice a repetition in the answers you get, or it may not feel like your reading at all.

There is a specific way to drink tea before reading tea leaves.

Prepare a cup of tea with any loose-leaf tea you wish. Some will have preferences for which kind clumps and makes formations easier, but you can do it with any tea you like. Drink your tea, and when there's one sip left, spin the teacup around and let the leaves spread around the whole cup. Then, drink your last sip and let the cup sit upside down until dry before interpreting it. The last sip of tea should be just enough liquid to allow the tea leaves to move as you spin your cup while leave groupings or clumps. These loose leaves or clumps will become the symbols you interpret. When you drink your last sip before turning the cup, hold the cup so the handle is facing down and drink from there. You can leave the cup on a saucer or cloth as it dries. Don't let it dry too long, though, because some of the leaves may dry and fall out.

The area around a cup handle represents love relationships.

When reading coffee grounds or tea leaves also make sure to pay attention to the sections of the cup itself. The handle is for love, the left side is for the present, the right is for the future, and the top and bottom of the cup are for money. It's important to use a cup that is pure white inside so you can truly see all the details of the leaves or grounds and the symbols they make. If the cup and saucer are stuck together by suction, the cup is called the "Prophet's Cup" and is actually a good sign that the intentions of the querent will come true.

Crystal balls help develop the clairs.

Clairs primarily refers to the abilities of clairvoyance, clairaudience, and clairsentience. The crystal ball has been made into a Hollywood cliche that portrays a message as detailed and accurate scenes of our lives that appear from within the depths of the crystal. This isn't how it works at all! The crystal ball is a focusing tool that helps you go deeper into a trance, and through deep meditative states you might access your clairvoyance—seeing an image in the ball or in your mind's eye. You might hear words and your clairaudience opens up. Almost anything can become a contemplation point, but a sphere in crystal is considered purer and more conducive to receiving messages.

You have a lifetime totem animal, as well as temporary ones.

We have one animal that walks with us for life, helping us understand our true nature, including our deepest needs and behaviors. We also have messenger totems that arrive once to show us a direction or alter our course of thinking. Journey totems can be with us during long chapters of our lives. They come and go when certain core themes arise and return again for another layer of learning. There are protector totems, healer totems, teacher totems, and shadow totems. When you can connect to and develop relationships with them, your life can change significantly for the better. You will be able to recognize very specific traits in yourself, as well as who is compatible with you, where you fit best with groups or work, and even what land or environment is best for you. If your totem lives in the mountains and you are stuck in a city, for example, that might be a sign that you would be better off moving to a smaller mountain town. Similarly, if your totem is a dog, then you'll need the people in your life to match your loyalty. In these types of situations, your totem, whichever one is present, can teach you how to correct this mismatch and shift your life.

Your health shows on your face.

Physiognomy correlates to Chinese medicine, and there are
points on the face and neck, or meridian lines, that correspond
to the organs and relate to your health. Bags under your eyes tell
you about the health of your inner organs. The bags under your
eyes are related to your kidneys, the space between and beside
your eyes is related to your liver, your upper cheeks represent
the stomach, the areas under your nose and above your eyebrows
represent the heart, the small intestine and nervous system
are represented by the forehead, and the large intestine is in the
groove between your nose and mouth. The bladder can be seen
in the sides of the face radiating from the eye to the hair line, and
the lungs can be seen in the jowl areas. Anything that shows up on
the face can symbolize a health issue, whether it's redness, acne,
moles, yellowish skin, or eczema. Whatever is on the outside is a
reflection of the inside and can show us where we need to heal.

In Chinese astrology, your birth year animal tells your true nature and your basic luck in life.

Each Chinese astrology sign is an animal and has personality traits, directions, elements, tastes, smells, and body parts, among other things, associated with it. Most people think that when it is their year, it will be lucky, but the Chinese consider a person's own year as a difficult one, especially for their health. The luck or misfortune of each year is determined by a few things: Is the current animal compatible with your own? Is the element of the year supporting you or draining you? Are the stars for that Chinese year helping you or hindering you?

There are twelve animals and five elements, so the full cycle of combinations takes sixty years to complete. It can get a bit complex to understand what your year might be like. For example, if you were born in 1999, you are an Earth Rabbit. If you want to see what 2020 was like for you, you would compare the Year of the Metal Rat with your sign. Earth is compatible with Metal but will draw energy from you instead of supporting you due to the cycle of the elements. The Rat and the Rabbit are not compatible in nature. Overall, this would have been a tough year, and Rabbits are generally considered to be a symbol of luck. The Dragon is considered the luckiest of all the Chinese animals.

In Chinese fate reading, one character in your fate reading shows your nature at a soul level.

The fate reading is a powerful divination tool where each element and animal of your birthday are put into a chart of eight overall characters. These are called the Four Pillars. For example, if you were born on July 6, 1967, your year and element are Yin Fire Goat. The symbol for Yin Fire is written on top of the symbol for the goat. You then take the same data for your month, day, and hour of birth and put them in the fate diagram. The element of your hour of birth shows your deepest self at the soul level, called the Heavenly Stem of the Daymaster. If your hour element is yang Metal—the strongest combination—then even if you are a sensitive Rabbit, you will be strong inside! The opposite is also true of course. Based on the relationships between that central element and all the other characters in the fate reading, they can tell your journey in life. If your Heavenly Stem is compatible with that of your partner, there will be a beautiful relationship bond.

The *I Ching* (*Book of Changes*) gives deep wisdom and reflection, not predictions.

Each verse in the *I Ching* is profound. There are some games that use it as a prediction tool, but the original writings of the trigrams come from a philosophy of nature that is a part of the entire Chinese system, including feng shui, acupuncture meridians, Chinese astrology, and fate reading. The entire system of health, space arrangement, medicine, and prediction is based on the elements of nature and their intricate interactions.

54

Wear a protective amulet to ward off the evil eye.

Belief in the evil eye crossed many lands and cultures for a very long time, including in Greece and Italy, and in Jewish, Hindu, Islamic, and Buddhist cultures. The belief is that someone can cast bad fortune on you with their eyes, curse you instantly, or even steal your soul. Most of those accused of casting the evil eye were malformed individuals, old women, childless women, and strangers, which goes to show you who they feared most back then. Most often it was thought to be malice or jealousy toward someone beautiful or prosperous that brought the evil eye to bear, to the point that it was not considered favorable to have your children be praised or possessions complimented. People would wear protective charms or hang garlic on their doors to avert it. There are even modern stories of grandmothers spitting in the faces of their beautiful grandchildren to ward it off. Overall, the main point behind the evil eye comes from the Bible in Matthew 6:22-23: "The eye is the lamp of the body. If your eyes are good, your whole body will be full of light. But if your eyes are bad, your whole body will be full of darkness. If then the light within you is darkness, how great is that darkness!" Basically, it is saying that envy and jealousy are destructive.

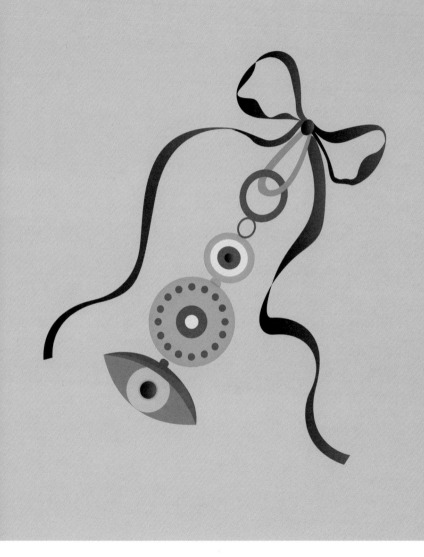

Using the medicine wheel balances all sides of your life.

There are the four sacred directions: east, west, north, and south. All four directions have specific meanings in your life. There are also four aspects to the wheel: mental, physical, emotional, and spiritual. Each of these must be in balance to have a healthy and happy life. Yellow is the east, red is the south, black is the west, and white is the north. Each color and direction have a season, element, planet, aspect of life, clan, and plant medicine. It is a complex and holistic system. The wheel or circle is very important in this life philosophy. The circle represents the circle of life, the circle of knowledge, and the circle of self-awareness. The seasons are a circle, and the spirit lives on and on into the spirit world. We need to use the medicine wheel to find this balance and live a happy life. It is a tool. The divinatory aspect comes from a reader or interpreter who will channel symbols to draw onto the medicine wheel for you. It can be any symbol and on any quadrant. Knowing the wheel is essential, but channeling is also essential.

Playing cards correlate to the Minor Arcana in the tarot.

There are fifty-six playing cards with ten of each suit and court cards. The tarot has seventy-eight cards due to the Major Arcana being added to it. Many will use the playing cards in a similar way to the Minor Arcana. Cartomancy relies less on symbolism and specific spreads. It's more about numerology and intuition. There are correlations between the tarot and playing cards. The Hearts are the Cups, the Clubs are the Wands or Batons, the Diamonds are Swords, and the Spades are the Pentacles or Disks.

Hold your pendulum gently in one hand with it dangling over your other palm.

Focus on a question that you know for sure has a "yes" answer. Something like, "My name is_____." Let the energy build and see what direction the pendulum moves. Pose a similar question that is a definite "no," such as "I am an astronaut" (unless you are!). See which way the pendulum moves. Now you have activated your pendulum to know its answers! When you ask your question, you need to simply focus on the question versus your desired outcome, and trust the "yes" and "no" the pendulum showed you in the test run.

Each pendulum can be different.

Some are metal, while some are quartz or made of other gems. Some will move in circles, while some will swing back and forth. You can also make a simple pendulum from a needle and thread! The motion itself, as well as the intensity of the motion, will often give you an indication of the answer. Whether the swing is emphatic or barely noticeable, it's up to you to trust your intuition when determining meanings. It's also worth taking your time to choose the pendulum that moves strongly for you so the answers are easier to interpret.

59

Create a random playlist for musical divination.

Canticumancy works by trusting that the music lines you hear when asking a question are speaking a truth. All of us have walked around singing or humming the same song on repeat like a mantra, or finding that a certain song feels like a theme for a relationship or chapter of our lives. If a song grabs your heart that deeply, the lyrics are certainly a mantra or prediction for your life. We can use this form of divination in a couple of ways. If you seek an answer, you can create a very random playlist to use, meditate on your question, and then pick a random song on the list and press play. See if any of the lines stand out to you about your situation.

Similarly, without any preparation, you can simply pay attention to any song you are hearing on repeat, either in your head or literally on a radio. If a song seems to be following you, there is a reason to listen to those lyrics! Song lyrics becoming mantras has a very powerful effect on our minds. If you walk around with angry or pessimistic lyrics in your head, they're going to color all your interactions with that world view, instead of a positive, inspirational, or even just a calm song. You can also glean a lot of information about a person by what they mainly listen to. It might show you some basic elements of compatibility if you are always listening to gentle acoustic music and they listen to heavy metal. Many times, when we don't have a way or the courage to communicate how we feel to others, songs can tell us. Does your girlfriend put on a certain song in your presence? Pay attention to it, even if she is doing it unconsciously. Music is truly the language of the soul and encompasses a deeper truth within it.

You must be extremely attuned to subtleties for dowsing to work.

Dowsing rods can be either a forked stick or two separate rods with a long metal stick pointer that swings and moves. In either case, the dowser (person holding the rods) must be super in tune with subtle sensations in order to find what they are looking for. There might be twitches in the rods or in your muscles, the rods might not align at first unless you are truly calm, and they may move and go crazy when there is a disturbance somehow. Many believe that the rods will crisscross or jerk downward when walking over a water source underground. People have used this form of divination since the European Middle Ages. Dowsing can be done to find water underground in order to drill a hole for a well or find tributaries from a river. They can be used to sense energies such as ley lines (energy lines that travel across the globe and are affiliated with certain deities) or to find portals. Dowsing rods can also be used to show a person's auric field or to find buried metal or gemstones.

In bibliomancy, focus your mind on a question, randomly open a book, and pick the first line you see.

This is your message. This one is fun and can be so uncannily accurate! You can do it one of two ways. The first way is to make your choice at random. Choose any book near you and flip it open without thinking of anything and put your finger on the first line you see. Read this as a message to yourself. Sometimes the line can take a bit of thought to interpret, but other times it can be incredibly spot-on! The second way is more intentional, but still random enough to give you a message. With this technique, you think of a specific question and then pick a page number and a line number, and *then* grab the first book beside you and look that up. For example, you ask, "Will I sell my house soon?" and choose page 25, line 4. Grab the closest book to you and find the page and line. Perhaps it's a cookbook and it says, "Let the mixture stand for 2 hours." This can easily be interpreted as waiting to sell, and perhaps the wait will be two weeks or two months. That's *one* way of interpreting it. Once again, you will need to trust your gut on interpretations.

You can use the flame or the wax formations for candle divination.

There are many ways to use candles for divination. We usually burn candles while doing other forms of divination to indicate that spirit is present or that the will (the flame) is active in the work we are doing. You can sit with the lit candle and gently gaze at the flame while asking for signs and symbols on a topic. The way the flame moves can give you your answer. If you first ask about a relationship and the flame takes a while to light, this initially tells you the energy of the relationship. If the flame jumps around, moving and swaying or flickering, it might tell you the relationship is very dynamic, is changeable instead of stable, and has excitement and some small conflicts.

Obviously, we all want a stable and strong flame where love is concerned. You can also use the wax formations to divine your answers. The melting of the wax, and its speed, shapes, and texture can all be symbolic. Once again, for a love question, if the candle melts quickly and is runny, the relationship may also be short-lived or burn out after a period of passion. If the wax burns more slowly, with only a few beads on it, we would usually expect a solid bond.

Stay away from Ouija boards!

Ouija boards are real—but the entities they conjure are *not* good. Many people report feeling very scared and disturbed by the spirit long after the experience is over. Lower spirits can speak, but why let them? They will usually say things that scare you and really aren't good for your mental health. Many people report having had difficulties in their lives that lingered for months or even years after bad experiences with a Ouija board.

Throw salt into a fire to see your future.

There are a few ways to divine with salt, but one in particular is very similar to pyromancy, a method in which a pinch of salt is thrown into a fire and the crackling and sparks are interpreted to get a sense of the future. The Scots used to do this every year on Imbolg night. Alternatively, salt has long been linked to purification and protection. It's still common to put salt in the corners of a room or around a property to protect and cleanse it. In ancient Egypt they used to pour salt onto a table and look at any patterns in the salt, with ridges meaning obstacles, and depressions in the salt meaning delays and disappointments.

When practicing capnomancy, heed the direction of the smoke.

Ancient Babylonians used this method of smoke divination, as did ancient Greeks and Celts. While observing the smoke from a fire, the direction of the smoke was very significant. A straight-up pure stream was thought to be the best omen, whereas plumes of smoke that touched the ground were thought to be a sign of urgent action needed. Animal sacrifices were made, and the smoke from the fire would be interpreted. Smoke has also been used for cleansing, clearing, and purifying throughout the centuries, so the smoke can also be interpreted to determine whether a space is clean or not. Now we mainly do this with incense or sage. Some of us might do it when we light a cigarette. What patterns and swirls does the smoke make when burning it? How can we interpret the images we see in it? Center yourself and ask your question, then light your incense or sage. If the smoke goes straight up, your answer is a "yes." If the smoke breaks up or looks uneven it would be a "no." If the smoke deviates and makes rings, your answer would be "yes," but things will not go as expected since it's not a straight line. You can also try to be more directive with the reading by asking that the smoke come toward you for a "yes," and away from you for a "no." Leave room to let symbols, faces, or numbers appear to you as well. It's endless what you can see!

66

Your fate is in your name.

The great Achilles won against Hector because the sum of the numbers in his name was greater. This is an example of onomancy. There are various ways to calculate it and it has changed with different cultures over the centuries. Priests used to be involved in naming children so they would have the best chances in life. The priests would consider the number of vowels, as well as the parents' names, in their decision. The Pythagoreans started this tradition, and said that if someone had an even number of vowels in their name there was an affliction on the left side of their body and, if uneven, there was something wrong on the right side—pretty much ensuring that no one was fine. Later on, they assigned a number to each letter and added them to get a value for one's personality. If you write the alphabet and place the numbers 1 to 9 underneath, repeating until you reach the end, you will be able to add your name. John would be $J = 1 + O = 6 + H = 8 + N = 5 = 20$, or 2, as a name significator. People with a 2 name are concerned with relationships and partnerships of all kinds and are said to be intuitive and diplomatic but also very changeable, often dealing with fears of being alone. You can add your own name and see what it tells you.

Handwriting shows our inner psychology.

Did you know that you can see if someone has an inflated ego by the way that they write? If the crossing lines of a "t" are either right at the top of the letter or above it, this person has a very high opinion of themselves. The contrast is true as well, if crossing the "t" too low. The same is true for dotting the "i." If letters lean to the back, it means a person is more introverted, while front leaners show a person has more interest in working with others. Applying heavy pressure when writing shows that one might be angry, while average pressure shows confidence and commitment. Soft pressure indicates a sensitive or shy person. If a signature can be read easily, it shows an open person, and if it's illegible the person might be someone who is hard to read. If letters are looped when writing, it shows openness and a feeling nature, while closed letters show a restricted or very private personality. If you look at the writing of famous people online, it is utterly fascinating.

While practicing libanomancy, make sure to observe the incense smoke as well as the ash for your message.

Prepare the room first by making sure there is nothing that can interfere, like an open window, a breeze, or a fan. If the smoke from your incense burns in a thin straight line upward, it means the room needs to be cleansed. Generally, smoke rising upward indicates a "yes," while broken streams or inconsistency are a "no." Cumulations of smoke can be interpreted as a "yes" as well. However, your intuition determines what you see in the smoke formations, whether it be faces, numbers, or symbols.

Automatic writing—keep your pen moving no matter what comes out.

Automatic writing means we are writing uncensored. It will look like gibberish sometimes, without full sentences, grammar, or even on the line of the page! The whole point is to keep your eyes focused on something like a candle flame or crystal ball, and not watch the page too much. Just keep your pen writing. Occasionally, you will hear breakthrough sentences, names, or places. You can't control what answers come in this method. Insights and sometimes predictions will arise in the midst of writing out whatever is in your head. This allows your clairaudience to develop, so you learn to relax and heed the words and phrases that come to you that don't really feel like your own. You might hear words in another voice or accent, or you may be in a trance and not hear anything, but the energy in the hand and pen are busy and keep writing. When you read it back to yourself afterward, you can highlight the things that stand out as insights or strongly phrased ideas. The next part is to live life and see if any of it is predictive over time. Sometimes you can be more directed in your automatic writing on a certain question. If you print it at the top of your page and keep your eyes gazing lightly on it as you allow your hand to just keep writing, it will be focused on the question versus a general session.

Color divination can be surprisingly revealing of our true emotions.

There are numerous ways to use color for divination, but mainly it is used to get the emotion and symbolism associated with that color as your answer to a question. If I take a set of colored pencils or cards, buttons, or ribbons, think of my question, then choose one color, that color will be my answer. There are also many varied meanings of colors in different traditions. For example, white is usually associated with purity, but in Chinese feng shui it is associated with the element of metal, the mental aspect of life, the lungs, the west direction, and grief. In the pagan tradition, it is associated with air or spirit and is the east direction. Purple for the Celts is associated with royalty, but in Greece it is associated with death. Color symbolism for pagans is slightly different than for First Nations. You need to choose which color tradition fits you best before you use it for divination so you don't confuse yourself. Each tradition often associates an emotion, a direction, bodily organs, planets, elements, and sometimes astrological signs or tarot cards with colors. This kind of reading can be more powerful than you think!

Let your intuition choose the right gemstone for you.

Gemstones have complex energies and meanings, and each individual stone is unique. It's important to hold the gemstones and notice the ways in which your body reacts. Pay attention to what images and thoughts come to you while holding them. You are reading the energy of these stones to determine the ones that are a good match for you. When there is a good vibration between you and a crystal, you can use it for divination.

Always cleanse and charge your crystals before divination.

When you buy a crystal in a shop, there will certainly have been many people who handled the crystal prior to you, leaving many energies in the crystal to clear. All you need to do is burn sage and rotate the gemstone in the smoke over and over until you feel the energy is lighter and the stone is brighter in color or feeling less heavy or sticky. You can also put your gemstones into a bowl of salt overnight and rinse them in the morning. To charge them you can leave them in the sunlight for a few hours or an entire day. Use your intuition to determine how long you should leave them. Your crystal will then be ready to open and receive only your energy or the divine energy you are connecting with.

Find a good crystal for gazing.

Believe it or not, most crystal balls are made of glass. If you want to use the same technique of scrying with gemstones, you need to find a crystal that is large enough, very clear and reflective, or has interesting formations within it that can aid your interpretation. A large smoky quartz could be perfect for this because there will be clear areas, smoky areas, and striations within it as well. If you want specific answers to certain themed areas of life, you can choose a gem that matches that. For example, if looking for general clarity, you might want clear quartz or even obsidian for going deeper into an issue. If you want to ask about love, then rose quartz is excellent, as is rhodochrosite since it is sometimes considered a higher octave of self-love. For questions about earthy matters, such as work or money, you can use jasper, tiger's-eye, or hematite. Some other favorite stones for gazing are labradorite, amethyst, and fluorite for spiritual questions, opening your third eye, and opening your intuition. Kyanite is excellent for aiding prophetic dreams. Moldavite is very popular of late, but we need to go easy with it. It is very powerful to remove negative energies around us, but it can also overwhelm us. Citrine and selenite are lovely and easy gems to use because they are full of light and never need cleansing. However, most do need cleansing. Whichever you choose, be sure to charge them, cleanse them if needed, pray on them if you wish, clear your mind of the question or purpose for the gazing, and allow your intuition to come through freely.

Nature-Based

There are omens in falling leaves.

If you are thinking of a question and pass by a tree, if a single leaf falls, you can interpret the speed and motion of the falling leaf, its color, and whether it falls face up or down, pointing toward you or not, and of course the symbolism of the specific tree. If you ask about love and an oak leaf falls, spinning rapidly to the ground, landing face down, we might deduce a sharp decline in that relationship—from solid and reliable (the mighty oak) to perhaps spinning out of control. If, on the other hand, you ask of love and two linden leaves fall before you facing each other and upward, you can perhaps say the relationship will become closer; linden trees symbolize truth and love with their heart-shaped leaves.

Every flower has a meaning.

If a lover gives you carnations instead of roses, it is indicative of innocence rather than romantic love. If roses are yellow as opposed to red, it indicates friendship more than romance. When you pick the petals of a daisy asking, "He loves me, he loves me not," you are practicing floromancy. There are many ways to use flowers for divination. If you want to know the quality of your current relationship with someone—no matter if romantic, platonic, or familial—you can go into a meditative state and ask to be shown a flower that represents the relationship. If you see red roses, this is a romantic bond with passion. If you see violets, the relationship indicates modesty and humility. This might be harder to interpret, but it could still be romantic and include these qualities. If you are shown a peony, it means good luck, prosperity, and honor. If you see a clematis in your meditation, it can sometimes mean artifice, therefore you might not trust this person fully. You can also do certain rituals with flowers to see the true nature of a relationship by placing two flowers that are in bud and about to bloom side by side, with the names of each person written on a paper resting beside each flower, and see how they behave as they bloom. The blooms might unfold at the same time or be very different, symbolizing the opening of the heart to each other. They might lean together or away from each other. Or they might even entwine, indicating a marriage or commitment.

Trees are omens.

You can interpret messages by way of twigs, fallen branches, shapes of trees, or burning wood. A fallen branch on your path might be interpreted as a message by the direction it points, whether it has its full bark or is bare, what kind of tree it is, and the symbolism of that tree. An oak branch facing you in full bark has a different message than a willow branch that has fallen in a curve. Twigs might have different shapes, point to objects on the path, have leaves or buds, or be dead wood. In each case they can be interpreted. When Franklin D. Roosevelt's mother died, the largest tree on the property crashed just after she took her last breath. Not everything is that clear!

But needless to say, we often get messages from trees. We all feel it when a tree around our home is cut down or damaged—there is a gap or disturbance in the energy. If a tree falls or is chopped down, you suddenly can lose a sense of protection or privacy you cherished. This proves there is great energy in the tree in the first place. In the art of feng shui, a master can tell if someone in the home will succeed or be ill by the health and placement of the trees around the home. We can also talk to trees. There is so much life in and around a tree to interpret. When asking a question, put your hand on its trunk and feel what it would say to you if it could. See if any little birds, squirrels, or other critters show up after you ask. See if the tree moves differently after your ask—perhaps a gust of wind goes through it or leaves suddenly float down to the ground. Everything can be interpreted for your question.

Divine your past, present, and future with lightning flashes.

Greeks, Babylonians, Etruscans, and Celts all practiced this art. The Greeks believed lightning bolts were thrown by the angry gods Jupiter and Poseidon. The intensity, sound, color, and closeness were all considered in the predictions. According to the Roman author Seneca, the heavens were divided to interpret the lightning, with the east side representing one's own people and the west side being the enemy. Today if we used lightning for divination, we could also pay attention to the direction it happens in with a different lens than friend or foe. Perhaps we can see it as a tarot card, with the left being the past and the right being the future, and right in front of us is certainly the present. If we see a lightning storm, we can ask a question and observe the skies. If the lightning is to the left and loud it can be a sign of past issues to resolve or someone from the past coming back strongly, for example.

Collect your stones naturally.

Gathering your own stones brings more spiritual power to the divination because those particular stones called to you somehow. You will need thirteen stones, and then you must assign them each a meaning. Try to select ones similar in size and shape. You can write your words or symbols on them or paint them. You can put them in a bag or a bowl, then ask your question and draw one to interpret. The most important thing of all is to trust your intuition and feel which stone's energy is strongest when asking the question. You can also do a more advanced version if you want to create a board for your stones to be thrown upon. If the board is blank, you might throw all thirteen stones and see how they land, connecting the story like dots on the board. You could also paint or draw on your board to create grids or a pie wheel of anything you wish to break down the reading.

Find a high vantage point—with clear skies.

Divination by nature is always amazing and reassuring because we know we can't manipulate it. If you want to get an answer from the clouds in the sky, it's good to be at a high vantage point, a lookout, or a flat open space so you can observe as much of the sky as possible. The colors matter, as do the shapes of clouds, their direction of movement, and whether they are low or high. If you ask, "Can my relationship with my brother become close again?" and you sit and observe two clouds drifting together in the same direction, that could be a "yes." You're going in the same direction, but closeness would need another aspect to see. If the two clouds touch at some point or if they are pink, this would be a good sign for a "yes." However, if one cloud is darker and looming higher than the other, it might show that one of you dominates the relationship instead of you being equals. You might see shapes in those same clouds as well. Animals are common to see, or faces and vehicles. Take all of the visual information into consideration for this answer.

Look to phenomena in the skies when in doubt.

The air element is closely connected to the spirit. The skies, wind, light, rainbows, and clouds are all emotional correspondences to hope and faith. If you are in despair about something and go for a walk after a rain shower only to see a double rainbow over the horizon, would you not take it as an uplifting sign? Winds and directionality, lightning patterns, thunder, shooting stars, and shapes of clouds all fit in this category, and there are so many subtle ways they can be interpreted. If you ask the skies to show you your answer about whether a love partner will enter your life soon, and you see a shooting star, you will be encouraged and feel the spark might ignite quickly. The love may enter with some surprise or eccentric aspect since you didn't expect this little starburst across the sky. If you further ask for a sign of how long this will take and you see a heavy cloud moving slowly, you will sense that it might be slow or take a while, and perhaps there are some heavy emotions (cloud ready to shed water!) in the way of your meeting this person. And yet the shooting star shows it could happen at any moment. Paying attention to all the subtle information will give you clear messages.

Meditate on a body of water.

There are many practices linked to hydromancy since water is so prevalent in life and represents so many things to us—from emotions to the collective unconscious of mankind. The patterns made by stones dropped into a river used to be interpreted as messages. The ancient Greeks believed nature spirits lived in fresh water, and many myths of great sea creatures exist all over the world. Most of the time hydromancy was about sitting in stillness to watch a river's patterns or to see the reflections in a clear bowl of water—similar to scrying. Messages from the gods would appear while gazing into the water. It was used by Nostradamus while he made his famous predictions. He sat with a clear bowl of water and watched for any movement or messages that came through to him, with amazing results.

Sadly, there are other, more horrific practices of hydromancy, such as determining if someone was a witch by throwing them into water to see if they would float. This practice was also done with newborns to see if they were illegitimate by the ancient Germanic cultures along the Rhine. We can all use water for divination, without the ancient barbaric practices. If you sit by a pool, a river, or the ocean and allow yourself to relax, over time the water will swirl or rush and have little inlets of calm water or differentiated colors, and you can interpret these or see what they evoke to you. It's a very calming way to access your clair abilities. The water is a focusing tool, like a crystal ball. If you want to try other ways to interpret messages in the water, you can ask a question and then drop pebbles into the water, observing the way the rings form and overlap each other. The patterns might bring up a message for you. You can also pay attention to anything floating along the water as a symbolic message. Often, it'll unfortunately be a soda can or trash that shouldn't be there, but it is thus a message. If you see any fish or wildlife as you gaze, they are also part of the message.

You are connecting to a deep ancestral energy when performing pyromancy.

Pyromancy is most likely the oldest of all forms of divination since humans needed fire for life itself to go on—keeping them warm and fed among other uses. Usually, the diviner would interpret the shapes in the flames at a ceremonial or sacrificial fire and foretell the fate of the village or people in question. Today you could do it with a simple candle flame or a campfire. You need to be clear concerning the answers you seek and then light your fire—safely! See what images seem to appear in the flames as symbolic messages. Allow the fire or candle to burn down to its own end naturally or you might interrupt the process and its magic. You can also interpret the smoke it makes when it extinguishes as a sign as well. A simple way to do pyromancy with a question would be to write the question on a small piece of paper, light it on fire in a container that is safe (metal or cast iron), and let it burn to nothing. Observe how fast or slow it burns and if it creates a flame or just smoke as it burns. See if any remnants remain, such as a part of the paper with one word on it. When you have your clarity of the message you can dispose of the ashes in a way that feels right to you to cleanse this problem from your mind. You can flush them, submerge them in water or sand, or empty them into the trash safely. Whatever feels like closure.

The air element speaks to you through feathers.

When you come across a feather on your path, you can glean a lot of potent information from it. What kind of bird is it from? What does that bird symbolize? What color is the feather? Use your color symbolism for an extra part of its message. What direction is it pointing? Maybe you need to walk there, or it's telling you where your next home will be. Some feathers appear from loved ones who have crossed over—it's one of many ways spirit can speak. Alternatively, you may choose to focus on the type of bird the feather came from, as it could speak volumes. If you were thinking about your boss and you suddenly see a blue jay feather on the ground, you can apply the blue jay traits to your boss and see if it gives you insight.

Bird cries can be omens.

This might sound like an unusual form of divination, but it's been practiced since ancient times by the Greeks and Romans. If you were lost in a wooded area and had no idea which way to walk, would you look to the skies and follow the flight of the birds to guide you? Would you listen for the call of a loud crow and go in that direction? Birds flying into a home foretells a death to come. Crows showing up in your life often means a big transformation is coming in the next year.

Many legends speak of birds that accompany the spirit into the next realm when we pass, so of course birds can come along to show us direction through flight, caw, or song. Cardinals often show up to indicate the spirit of a loved one who has crossed over. If you encounter any bird directly, it is an omen, and you have to decipher what that bird means. Herons, for example, are rare to sight, so if you do notice one, it is a sign to follow its wisdom, which consists of stillness, self-sufficiency, and precision. Every bird is there to show you something.

Intuitive Abilities

Any reflective or illuminated surface can be used for scrying.

Whether you gaze softly into a crystal ball, a black mirror, fire flames, or a foggy windowpane, you can relax your gaze and see images. You can relax and bring yourself into a more meditative state and then ask a simple question you'd like an answer to. The trick is to stay relaxed and open. Allow your eyes to be easy and softly focused on the scrying surface, and as you do this there will be images that you see in your mind's eye or literally dancing in the candle flame or light reflected in patterns on a mirror. The images might be literal—seeing a person you know—but more often they will be symbolic, and you will need more time to process what the symbol might mean.

Yes, some dreams are predictive.

If it's your average dream, where one place shape-shifts into another and it's jumbled but it all feels meaningful, it's probably something to unpack with a good therapist. If on the other hand your dreams flow like a calm, clear sequential slice of life, it might be predictive. There are books you can find with lists of hundreds of dream interpretations to help you figure out the symbolic meanings—flying dreams meaning you are overcoming obstacles, teeth falling out showing a loss in your life, or dreams of being naked in public signifying that you might be feeling very vulnerable and exposed.

Predictive dreams are something else. They are more likely to be a snapshot of a typical day or place. You might dream that you were going to leave to get the groceries when you realized you forgot your keys, went back into the house, and the dog escaped. That feels mundane, but you'll wake up with this vivid and step-by-step story. Very often these kinds of dreams happen. Forgetting keys and dogs getting loose isn't a sexy prediction, but sometimes the boring dream sequence might be that you see yourself signing papers in an office and then regretting it when you leave, knowing in the dream there will be problems after this. It's foreshadowing an accurate aspect to you. Other things will be more specific, but the dream will feel like a clear, sequential story.

Pay attention to signs of spirit contact.

There are so many ways spirits communicate with us, both the good ones, such as loved ones and guides, as well as the not-so-nice ones, like disincarnated souls and entities. Entities will show up as a chill in the air when there is no wind, lights flickering on and off, areas of clutter we never want to go near, or a closet that will never close, among other things. Some entities will move objects around and knock things off shelves or attempt to touch you and attach to you. This might sound cool to some people, but living it is another story that is usually unpleasant or downright scary.

By contrast, when positive spirits contact us, they can often come in the form of birds; cardinals are a popular way. They can come through as a beautiful scent of flowers or the person's perfume. Some will come through with songs that suddenly play or books that drop off a shelf and lead you to something meaningful. Many make contact with us through dreams. And of course, many make contact with us through mediums. The biggest difference between the different types is the way you feel when it happens. Lower entities or those who are stuck on the material plane will have a heavy, tired, or depressing energy. Something might feel spooky or mysterious and intrigue you, but overall, it is energy draining. Spirits that are here to connect or guide you will come with that feeling of light as well and leave you feeling clearer, more loved, more connected, and better overall.

Stand in front of a white background for best results when aura reading.

In order to perceive the colors around another person's aura, it is necessary to have a neutral backdrop. If you do it in public with people or objects in your line of vision, they will influence what you see. White is the most neutral and will allow you to easily see the color reflecting upon it. Auras have many colors, which can fluctuate with different emotions and moods. You will see a range of colors around the body, and each color in each area will mean something. Seeing a grayish-yellow color around the stomach might mean a stomachache, IBS, or low self-esteem. A clear violet color around the head indicates a spiritual and intuitive person because the crown chakra is open and clear. You can use the chakra color system to interpret colors or the color meanings of your culture.

You can ask your deceased loved ones for answers.

Your relationship to your deceased loved one is best if it's based on love and a strong sense that they are okay on the other side. You don't want to become dependent on them for answers, so asking them where to park while out shopping may not be the best practice to respect that relationship. However, when it comes to deep matters of the heart, you can ask them to come through and guide you. If you are facing a dark night of the soul and truly can't decide what's best, it's okay to ask your loved one to give you a sign to make it clear—whether it's a symbolic answer or they show up in a dream that makes things more apparent. If you ask things that are not so serious or heartfelt, such as what movie to go see or whether a boyfriend will call you, then it's best to hold back because you could activate a trickster or lower entity with that energy since those are questions we tend to ask when anxious or in a more addictive/craving state of mind. To ask your loved ones for their guidance from the other side, you need to be centered and patient and show gratitude to them, then stay open for whatever comes. It might be very subtle, but you will intuitively know it's them.

Psychometry works best when you hold the object between both hands.

Psychometry is really fascinating. If you realize every object carries a vibration and story emitted from the owner and history of it, then you have to be open to the fact that everything has energy. Anything you wear, use, or keep with you is marinating in your vibrations, and it can be perceived in the object by a good intuitive. It's easier to focus and feel the object if it can be held between both hands instead of openhanded. Surrounding the object helps you feel all the angles and encloses it so it's not influenced by anything else around you. As you hold the object there are a few things to focus on to help the reading flow. Tune into its textures and temperature. Does it give you any sensation or image? Do any words come to mind? You can play with it, move it around, or put it on if you wish; a ring, bracelet, or watch can be powerful to wear to pick up its vibrations. If you don't know who it belonged to, try to imagine the qualities of the person you feel and describe them. If the object is an antique, you can ask yourself who originally wore it? Do you get any sense of whether the person you're currently sitting with bought it, or was it passed down, gifted to them by someone? All of these kinds of questions can open you up to channeling and bring images, words, or sometimes a movie clip to mind. Try to describe everything that comes up so the sitter can confirm it to you or not.

Real clairvoyance comes in the form of a flash image.

Sometimes you get random flash visuals that instantly give you fear or excitement. Other times you get a photobomb effect. A person's face walks across your brain as you're doing dishes, or you flash a door to a library as you're on your evening walk. You think nothing of it; it's more like a "hmmm, that's weird." This is usually the true clairvoyance moment. Clairvoyance comes with no emotion when it's real or predictive. That person's face you saw might be someone you know, and they will call you or drop in to see you soon. That library door might be a message to go in and be drawn to a book you need. Clairvoyance isn't meant to be an instant answer. It can be, but most often it's a partial clue to follow through on.

There is a big difference between clairaudience and hearing voices.

Hearing a little word or nudge in your mind is a pretty normal part of life if you listen to it. You might dialogue with yourself and talk to yourself—normal right? "Oh right, I can't park here . . . okay then, oh! There's a spot!" Who are we talking to? You could say it's your own higher self. Hearing the inner voice of intuition is similar. You may hear a name or a word or a direction. When you heed the voice, things turn out very well. Over time if this is the way you receive your intuition most, you might start hearing phrases or an inner voice that seems not to be yours. Usually, this will be positive and nondirective. Sometimes it could also be your spirit guide. In other cases, hearing voices is associated with mental illness. What's the main difference? The person hearing the phrase or voice feels the source as positive, supportive, and distant instead of bossy, invasive, and repetitive, and knows they have a choice to listen or not.

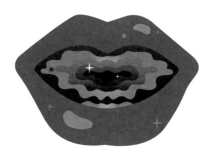

Clairsentience is the ability to feel information as a bodily sensation, so remember that not all body sensations are yours.

It's the queasy feeling in your stomach when something is off in the environment or with a relationship dynamic. It's the shivers you get when something that's said is true or if there's a spirit around you. It's the way your nervous system knows who is right for you by calming down or going haywire. You know who is truly listening to you by bodily sensations as well as so many other things. Sometimes, though, beyond your own alert systems such as these, you can pick up the body and mind states of others directly. You might have back pain when sitting next to someone else who is suffering from it. You might get a headache out of nowhere because there is a negative energy in a building, when you were just fine before you walked in. We all have the ability to experience the sudden sensations of others and of our environment, and for many of us, even community and global energies. All of our sensations are signs that can be interpreted. Sometimes a headache is just indigestion, but sometimes it's a haunted house! It's all very personal and subtle, but it's worth asking yourself what your sensations mean.

Take ample time to build a relationship with your spirit guides.

Just like any relationship you have in life, it takes time to get to know spirit guides well enough to recognize them anywhere. Friends eventually show us the way they like to speak and show up for us, and spirit guides are no different. It's easy to crave this kind of support in our lives and get confused or even tricked into believing that anything we sense or hear is the true voice of our spirit guides. This is why it takes time to know them—undeniably—and to listen to what comes through because it often isn't what you want to hear or see in the moment. There is a cultural perception or myth that spiritual guidance will always be reassuring or 100 percent clear on what to do next, but this isn't true. Your guides may alert you to let go of someone you desperately wish to be with if it's not for your highest good. So, the message will be painful to hear even if it is true. This is why it's so important to take time to get to know your spirit guides as consistent and recognizable energy that guides you positively and accurately on smaller things before trusting the messages that are harder to follow.

The spinning vortexes along our center energetic line through the body have power to reveal many answers to us.

Many sources cite the chakras as spinning wheels inside of us, but in truth they are conical and go from the front through to the back of the body. This can change the perception and how to work with them. You can visualize these any time you wish if you learn their precise locations, colors, and directions. If you can visualize each chakra open from front to back with the right color and direction, then this chakra or area of your life is in balance. When you can't see this, it tells you the wide range of issues you can work on. If your throat chakra is balanced, seeing a royal blue color in the center of the throat that goes through from front to back, then your communication is in balance. You say things at the right time to the right person with the right intensity. You speak from the heart, and you listen with compassion. When it's not in balance you get a sore throat, thyroid issues, and jaw pain, and hold in your feelings, overanalyze things, and become passive-aggressive because your heart and head are at war and you aren't communicating honestly. The list goes on! Each chakra is rich and complex and can help with just a visualization to know!

Mirrors are a gateway between you and the spirit world.

Mirror gazing is part of scrying. It's important to always remember that what you are doing is going deeper within yourself to access your clairvoyance ability in order to see signs and symbols in the mirror. Some people used to consecrate the mirror before using it to divine their answers. Even Nostradamus used mirrors when making his predictions. You might see light patterns, cloudy energies, or something in yourself morph, like seeing your face shape-shift slightly. Sometimes you will see sparkles, light orbs, symbols like hearts or flowers, or birds or cats, and sometimes you might see someone standing behind you as if they're right there!

Body Divination

Your luck shows on your forehead.

Part of Chinese face reading includes interpreting the wrinkles on your forehead. Most people will have three lines—the Heaven Line, the Man line and the Earth line. If you don't have any lines, it shows that you will receive a lot of help easily from people, are purer minded, and are lucky. If you have only two lines, it shows you don't feel much responsibility toward their family. If your lines are crooked or curved, it indicates accidents, and if the lines are straight then you have superior calm and patience in life.

The whole body is represented in the foot.

Whether it is Chinese medicine or reflexology, all the body parts and organs are represented on the foot and can be read and assessed. If you have a mole on the big toe or a callus on the heel, swelling or discoloration on the ball of the foot, or pain in the arches, it all means something about your inner organs and how healthy you are. Other things can be seen about your character from your feet as well. For example, if your big toe is longer than the rest of your toes, it means you are a clever and creative thinker. The longer your second toe, the more leadership qualities you have. If you are unhappy with loved ones it will show up as a curled fourth toe. People with wide feet are grounded and like to be busy, while those with long, narrow feet want to be pampered and can delegate the work to others. You will need training before you can give a good foot reading to someone, especially since health is involved.

Personology can show your character through face reading.

There is a tradition called personology that shows character traits by face reading, and there is physiognomy, which shows the health of a person by face reading. Personlogy can tell us that your deep-set eyes mean you have an intense and inquisitive, observant nature, while your thin upper lip can show that you have a hard time reciprocating in relationships. The overall shape of your face can say whether you are more sensitive and imaginative, or if you are a born leader or status seeker.

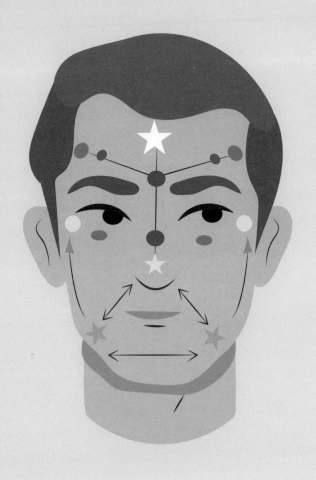

Moles can be omens.

There are a couple of different ways to regard mole reading. One is to look at your health based on where the mole is on the Chinese meridian lines. You can also interpret them by the color, size, and whether they are hidden or visible. It is said that a round mole with a bright color is a good omen, while a gray or yellowish one with an unusual shape is not auspicious. Moles on the head are excellent luck, although hard to see unless you are bald. Moles on the forehead are said to be average luck with weak family relationships and little support. Moles on the cheeks can suggest lawsuits but a generally upbeat and independent person, unless the mole is not a good color or shape, then the person might have social troubles. Moles on the chin that are gray or misshapen indicate instability of jobs, residences, etc. A good mole between the eyebrows can indicate great career success. There are so many more things to see with mole reading, but you get the idea! The other way is to see if any moles fall along the meridian lines and points. If you have a mole on Bladder 57 point for example, it means something very particular to your health and its causes.